Beginners' Programme
to
Plectrum Guitar
(Grade-3)

Beginners' Programme *to* Plectrum Guitar

(Grade-3)

By

Kapil Srivastava

(Guitarmonk)

UNICORN BOOKS

Publishers
UNICORN BOOKS
F-2/16, Ansari Road, Daryaganj, New Delhi-110002
☎ 23275434, 23262683, 23262783 • Fax: 011-23257790
E-mail: info@unicornbooks.in • *Website:* www.unicornbooks.in

Distributors
Pustak Mahal®
J-3/16, Daryaganj, New Delhi-110002
☎ 23276539, 23272783, 23272784 • Fax: 011-23260518
E-mail: info@pustakmahal.com • *Website:* www.pustakmahal.com

Sales Centres
- 10-B, Netaji Subhash Marg, Daryaganj, New Delhi-110002
  ☎ 23268292, 23268293, 23279900 • Fax: 011-23280567
  E-mail: salespmahal@airtelmail.in, rapidexdelhi@indiatimes.com
- 6686, Khari Baoli, Delhi-110006
  ☎ 23944314, 23911979
- Bengaluru: ☎ 080-22234025 • Telefax: 080-22240209
  E-mail: pustak@airtelmail.in • pustak@sancharnet.in
- Mumbai: ☎ 022-22010941, 022-22053387
  E-mail: rapidex@bom5.vsnl.net.in
- Patna: ☎ 0612-3294193 • Telefax: 0612-2302719
  E-mail: rapidexptn@rediffmail.com
- Hyderabad: Telefax: 040-24737290
  E-mail: pustakmahalhyd@yahoo.co.in

ISBN 978-81-7806-224-2

Edition: January, 2011

Printed at : Param Offsetters, Okhla, New Delhi-110020

Preface

I have great pleasure to bring forth this book as part of my endeavour to give some sort of organisation and structure to the music education in India.

Going by my professional experience in the last two decades, I have realized that India badly needs an organized music teaching system. The non-existence of such a system is one of the factors that plagues music education in our country. Non-compulsory music education and lack of awareness are the other factors which add to its present state.

This is the first book of the four volume book series published under the same title. As there is a dearth of constructive content for study and reference on this subject, to a great extent, this book will serve the purpose. The well organized content and the exercises of this book are a first-class study material for the aspiring students of music to prepare for various examinations. Even a 5 year old learner can use this book and it will help him to achieve the desired goal in a short span of time.

It is a matter of great pride and pleasure to note that my other books on music are well received by students and readers alike across the globe. They are also introduced as text books in many schools. We reach out all the places and regions through these books and thus we would be able to serve you without our physical presence.

I thank readers, students and others for their support and patronage. Your suggestions and comments on the further improvement of this book will be thankfully acknowledged and the same will be incorporated in the next edition.

Author

Overview

THE OBJECTIVES

The primary objective of this book is to familiarise the learners with terminologies, exercises and repertoires along with the audios of the compositions. This would help the learners to get a clear perspective on various aspects of the subject.

WHOM IS THIS BOOK FOR?

The book is for complete beginners who know nothing about the instrument, the students who prepare for examinations and the teachers who train the students.

THE SPECIAL FEATURES

- It is customized into levels and can be covered very easily in 12-24 sessions maximum based on time involvement.
- It is an ideal book for teachers who help their student in constructive sessions and productive outcome.
- The book is a step-by-step guide which takes a student from one level to the next. It also inspires success at every grade via achievements which motivates students to get curious and interested in further learning.
- This book contains an audio-CD that instructs on speed and movement of tune: and it is a good reference for the learners who find difficulties in staff reading.
- It contains the basics of staff notations which is very useful information for any music beginner.
- It is a compilation of very significant compositions, rated at a global standard, essential for any music student.

- It offers finger movements which are the most important part for a quality and right learning and support to both teacher and student.
- It offers exercise, pop music repertoire, music theory and Practice Compositions

HOW WILL THIS BOOK HELP YOU?

- It can help you in going about a step-by-step and systematic learning
- A quality and constructive repertoire of songs for your personal performance.
- It instructs you on finger patterns, so as to help both teacher and student with accurate fingering.
- You can expect a basic performance from yourself and can render a medley of tunes on any platform after practicing the given tunes.
- It can assist you, to a great extent, for a performance preparation and content and, thus, it can bring out a musician in you.

Content

EXERCISES

TECHNICAL DEVELOPMENT

(An essential practice for every music student)

Exercise - 17

Left Hand Exercises

(Finger Control Exercises - 2)

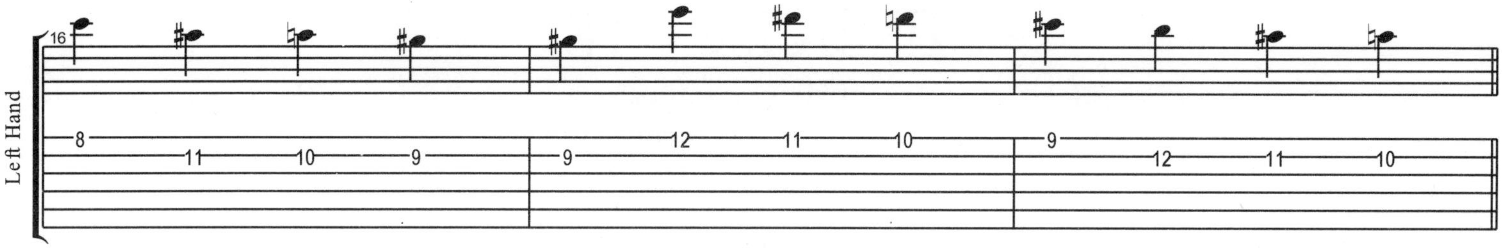

Going Back..

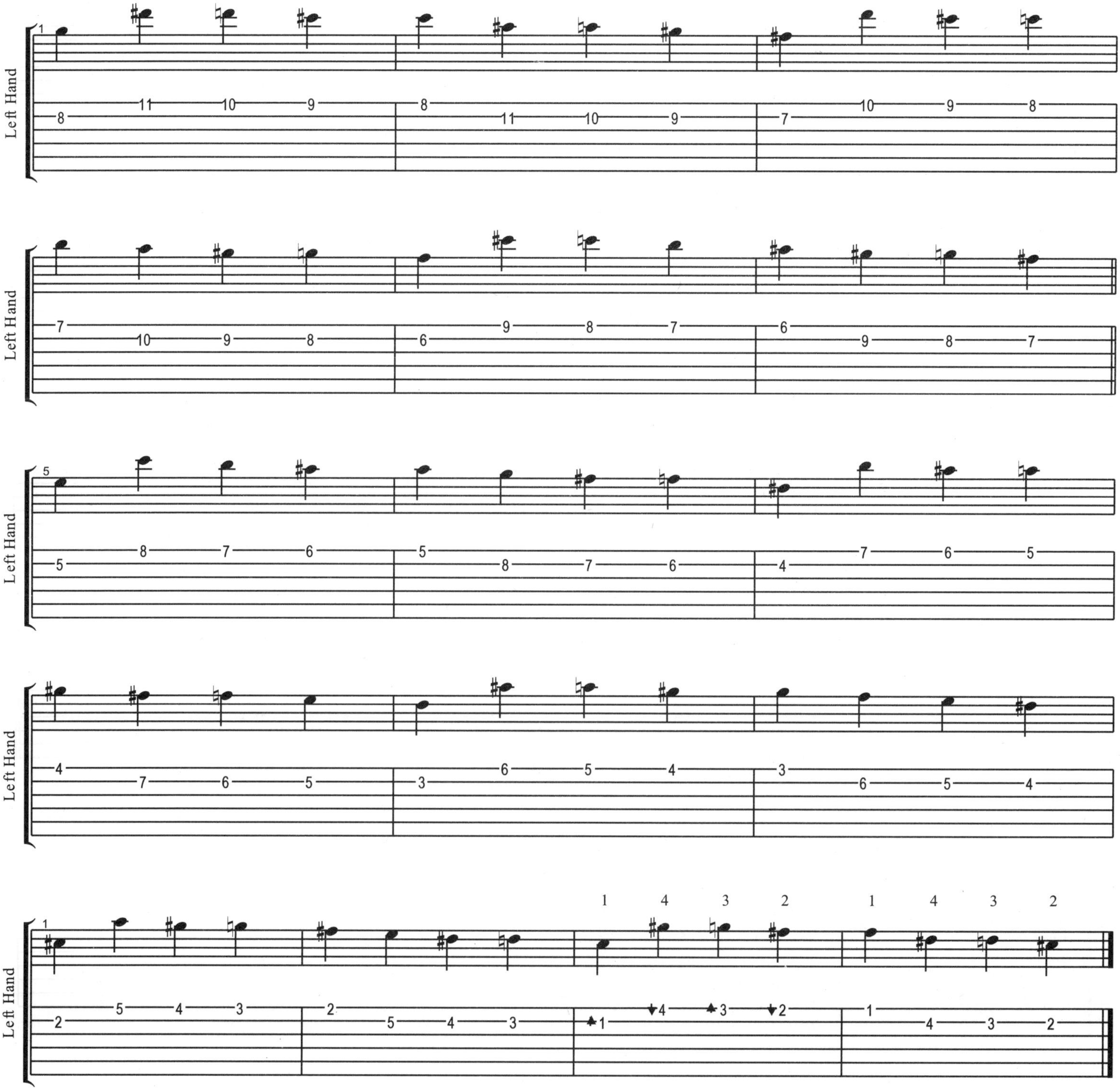

Exercise - 18

Left Hand Exercises

(Ladder Exercises, 2 String Ladder)

Left Hand
Left Hand
Left Hand
Left Hand

Exercise - 19

Left Hand Exercises

(Ladder Exercises, 4 String Ladder)

Going Back..

Exercise - 20

Left Hand Exercises

(Ladder Exercises, 4 String Ladder - 2)

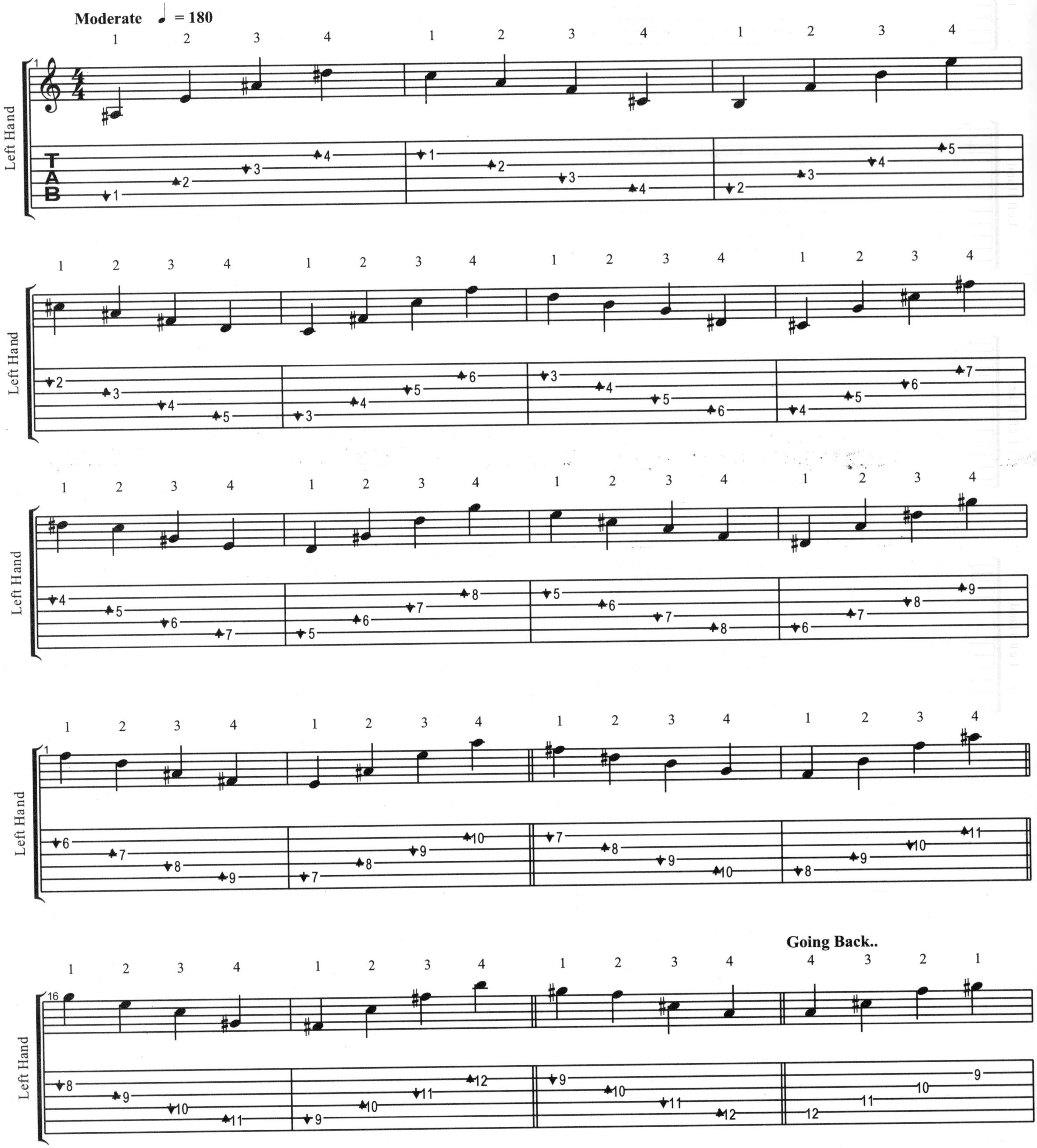

Left Hand
Left Hand
Left Hand
Left Hand

Exercise - 21

Left Hand Exercises

(Ladder Exercises, 4 String Ladder - 3)

Going Back...
Left Hand

Exercise - 22

Left Hand Exercises
(Ladder Exercises, Alternate String)

21
Left Hand
25
Left Hand
29
Left Hand
33
Left Hand

Scale Patterns & Exercises

> *"The Following exercises are also applicable for all instruments"*

Single Stroke (Tempo: 80)

Ascent:	C	D	E	F	G	A	B,	Ċ	
Descent:	Ċ,	B	A	G	F	E	D	C	(X 8 times)

Double Stroke (Tempo: 80)

Ascent:	CC	DD	EE	FF	GG	AA	BB,	ĊĊ	
Descent:	ĊĊ,	BB	AA	GG	FF	EE	DD	CC	(X 8 times)

Triple Stroke (Tempo: 80)

Ascent:	CCC	DDD	EEE	FFF	GGG	AAA	BBB,	ĊĊĊ	
Descent:	ĊĊĊ,	BBB	AAA	GGG	FFF	EEE	DDD	CCC	(X 8 times)

Quadruple Stroke (Tempo: 80)

Ascent:	CCCC	DDDD	EEEE	FFFF	GGGG	AAAA	BBBB,	ĊĊĊĊ	
Descent:	ĊĊĊĊ,	BBBB	AAAA	GGGG	FFFF	EEEE	DDDD	CCCC	(X 8 times)

Altered Stroke Patterns (Tempo: 80, Pattern - 1)

Ascent:	C	DD	E	FF	G	AA	B,	ĊĊ	
Descent:	Ċ,	BB	A	GG	F	EE	D	CC	(X 8 times)

Altered Stroke Patterns (Tempo: 80, Pattern - 2)

Ascent:	C	DDD	E	FFF	G	AAA	B,	ĊĊĊ	
Descent:	Ċ,	BBB	A	GGG	F	EEE	D	CCC	(X 8 times)

Altered Stroke Patterns (Tempo: 80, Pattern - 3)

Ascent:	C	DDDD	E	FFFF	G	AAAA	B,	ĊĊĊĊ	
Descent:	Ċ,	BBBB	A	GGGG	F	EEEE	D	CCCC	(X 8 times)

Altered Stroke Patterns (Tempo: 80, Pattern - 4)

Ascent:	C	DD	EEE	FFFF	G	AA	BBB,	ĊĊĊĊ	
Descent:	Ċ,	BB	AAA	GGGG	F	EE	DDD	CCCC	(X 8 times)

Triplet Stroke (Tempo: 80, Pattern - 5)

Ascent:	C-C	D-D	E-E	F-F	G-G	A-A	B-B,	Ċ-Ċ	
Descent:	Ċ-Ċ,	B-B	A-A	G-G	F-F	E-E	D-D	C-C	(X 8 times)

Scale Progression Exercises (Pattern – 1)

Ascent: C D E, D E F, E F G, F G A, G A B, A B Ċ

Descent: Ċ B A, B A G, A G F, G F E, F E D, E D C (X 8 times)

Scale Progression Exercises (Pattern – 2)

Ascent: C D E F, D E F G, E F G A, F G A B, G A B Ċ

Descent: Ċ B A G, B A G F, A G F E, G F E D, F E D C (X 8 times)

Scale Progression Exercises (Pattern – 3)

Ascent: C D E F G, D E F G A, E F G A B, F G A B Ċ

Descent: Ċ B A G F, B A G F E, A G F E D, G F E D C (X 8 times)

Scale Progression Exercises (Pattern – 4)

Ascent: C D E F G A, D E F G A B, E F G A B Ċ

Descent: Ċ B A G F E, B A G F E D, A G F E D C (X 8 times)

Scale Progression Exercises (Pattern – 5)

Ascent: C D E F G A B, D E F G A B Ċ

Descent: Ċ B A G F E D, B A G F E D C (X 8 times)

Scale Progression Exercises (Pattern – 6)

Ascent: C E, D F, E G, F A, G B, A Ċ

Descent: Ċ A, B G, A F, G E, F D, E C (X 8 times)

Upper Neighbor Exercise

Ascent:	C	D	E	F	G	A	B,	Ċ	
Descent:	Ċ,	B	A	G	F	E	D	C	
Ascent:	DC	ED	FE	GF	AG	BA	ĊB,	ĊḊ	
Descent:	ḊĊ,	ĊB	BA	AG	GF	FE	ED	DC	(X 8 times)

Lower Neighbor Exercise

Ascent:	C	D	E	F	G	A	B,	Ċ	
Descent:	Ċ,	B	A	G	F	E	D	C	
Ascent:	ḄC	CD	DE	EF	FG	GA	AB,	BĊ	
Descent:	BĊ,	AB	GA	FG	EF	DE	CD	ḄC	(X 8 times)

Lower + Upper Neighbor Exercise-1

Ascent:	C	D	E	F	G	A	B,	C	
Descent:	C,	B	A	G	F	E	D	C	
Ascent (L.N):	BC	CD	DE	EF	FG	GA	AB,	BC	
Descent (U.N):	DC,	CB	BA	AG	GF	FE	ED	DC	(X 8 times)

Lower and Upper Neighbor Exercise-2

Ascent:	C	D	E	F	G	A	B,	C	
Descent:	C,	B	A	G	F	E	D	C	
Ascent:	B**C**DC	C**D**ED	D**E**FE	E**F**GF	F**G**AG	G**A**BA	A**B**CB,	B**C**DC	
Descent:	D**C**BC,	C**B**AB	B**A**GA	A**G**FG	G**F**EF	F**E**DE	E**D**CD	D**C**BC	(X 8 times)

Points to consider for Exercise Practice -

- Tempo Selected in all exercises are considered for basic development and can be enhanced, customized based on student and teacher understanding.
- It's advisable to perform each exercise in presence of a senior or teacher to understand logic behind each exercise and achieve development.
- Some exercises are mentioned for 8 bars to demonstrate the importance of a single exercise in achieving finger dexterity. Student should repeat those exercises multiple times to achieve fluency.
- Student shouldn't jump to next exercises without achieving accuracy in the previous ones.
- The standard Guitarmonk Methodology adapted in practice (@ Guitarmonk Centres) is
    - Repeat a pattern atleast 8 times in a pre-defined tempo (speed)
    - Consider 8 repetitions as 1 round. Take atleast 8-10 rounds per exercise.
    - Take 8 rounds minimum without any error to move on to next exercise.
    - Increase speed to gain more confidence, control and take 8-10 rounds.

COMPOSITIONS

(A collection of special practice repertoire...)

Jingle Bells

Plectrum Guitar

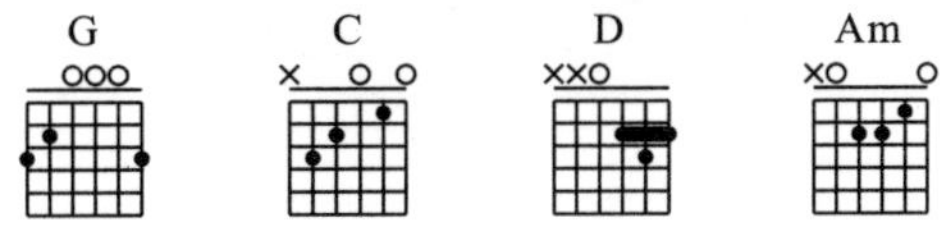

Melody
Chords
G G G C C D
G G G G G G

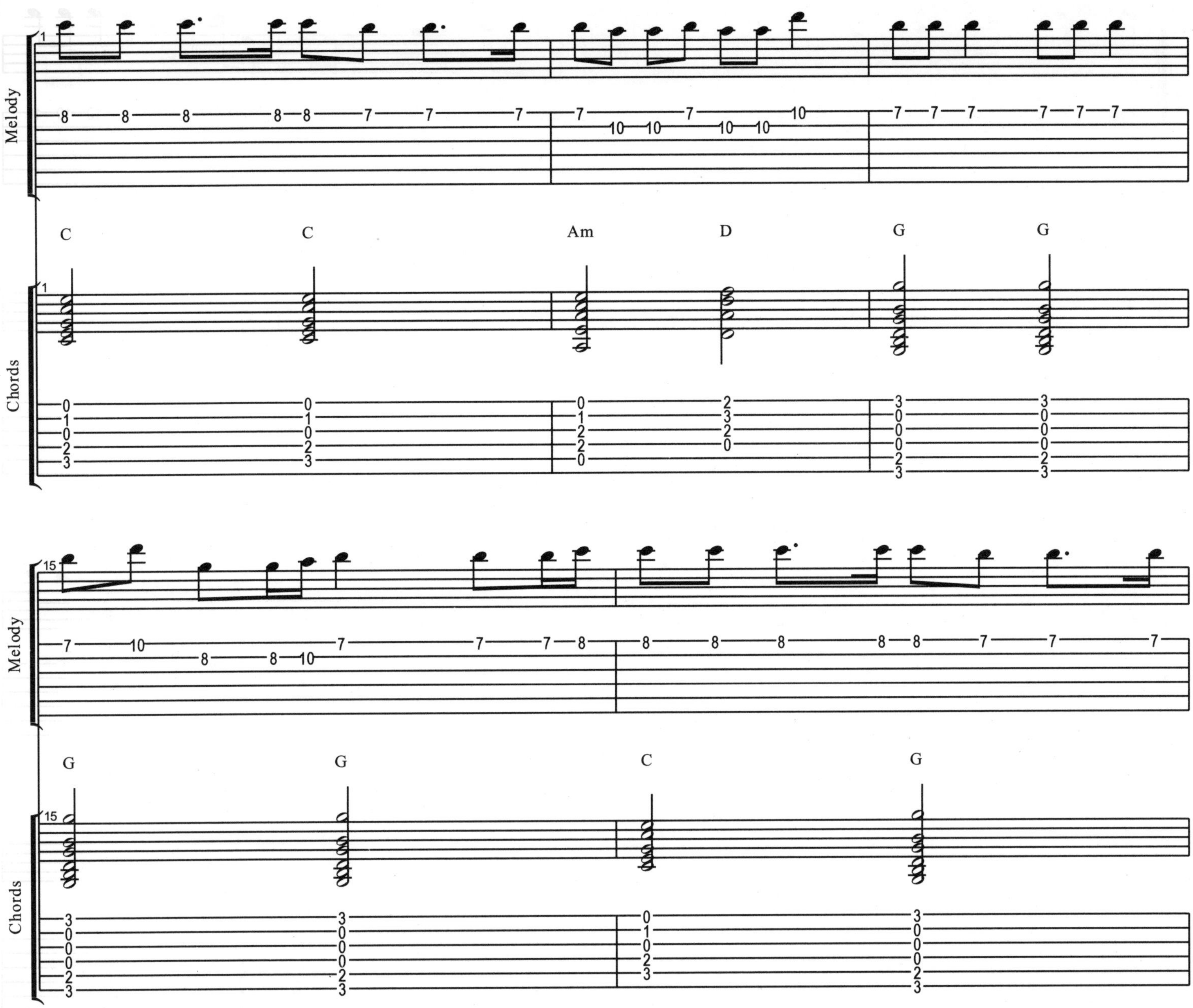
Melody
Chords
C C Am D G G
G G C G

Melody
D G G G
Chords
Melody
G C C D D G
Chords

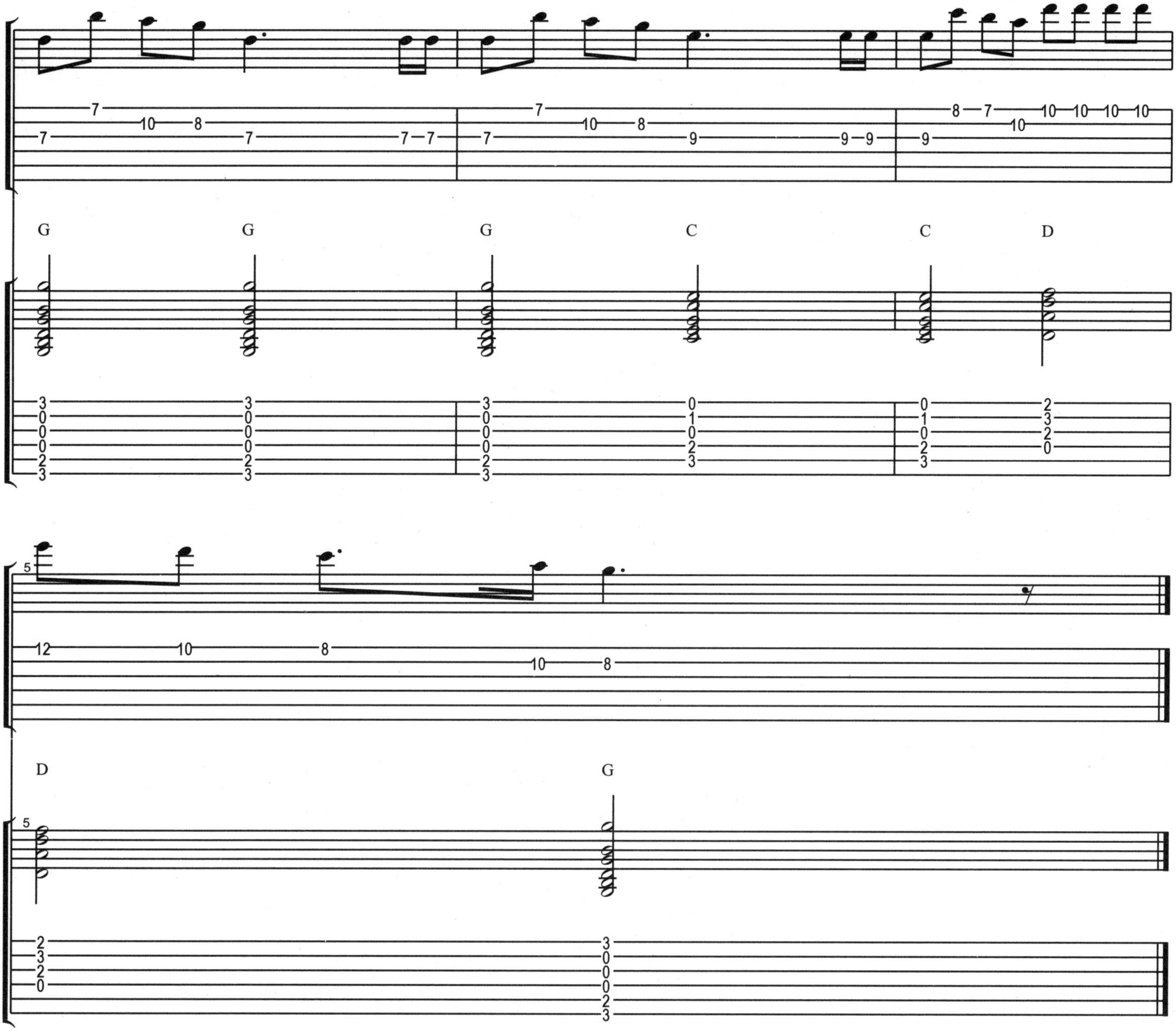
Melody
Chords
G
G
G
C
C
D
5
Melody
D
G
5
Chords

No Matter What

Plectrum Guitar

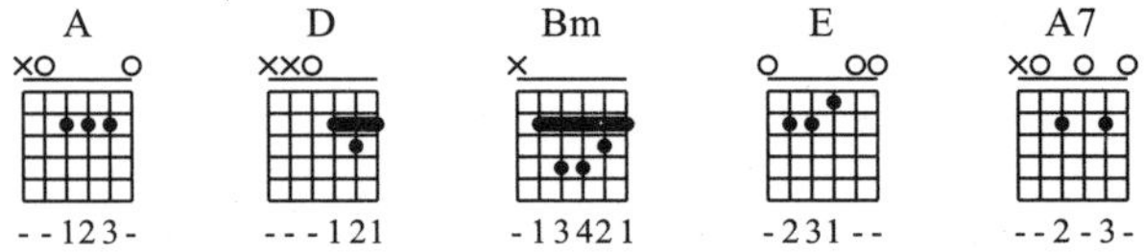

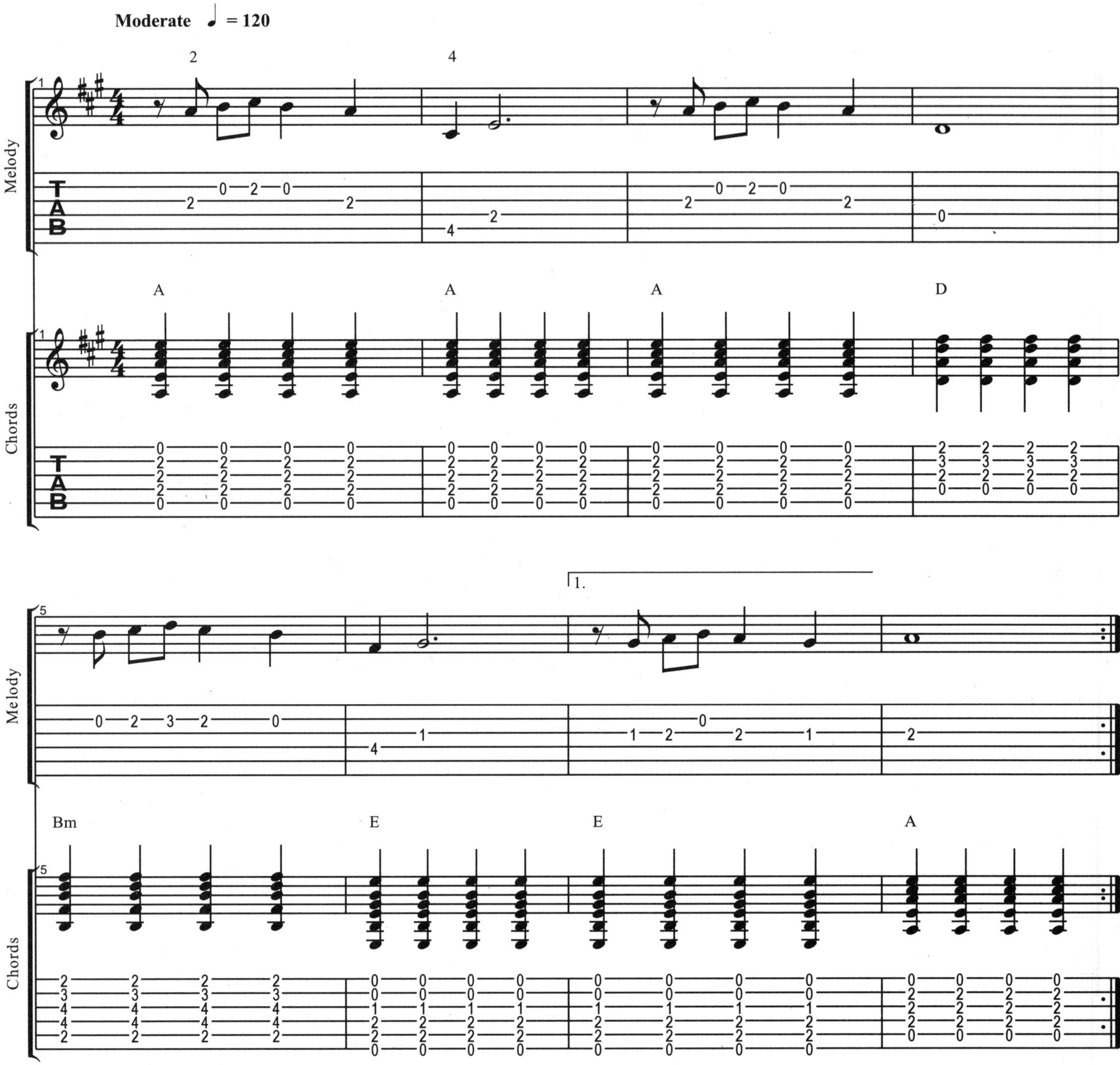

2.
Melody
Chords
A A A7 A
A D Bm E
E A

Rose on the Health

Plectrum Guitar

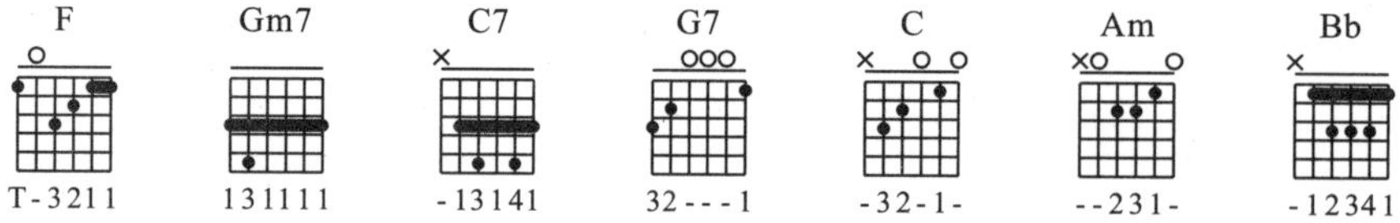

Moderate ♩ = 108

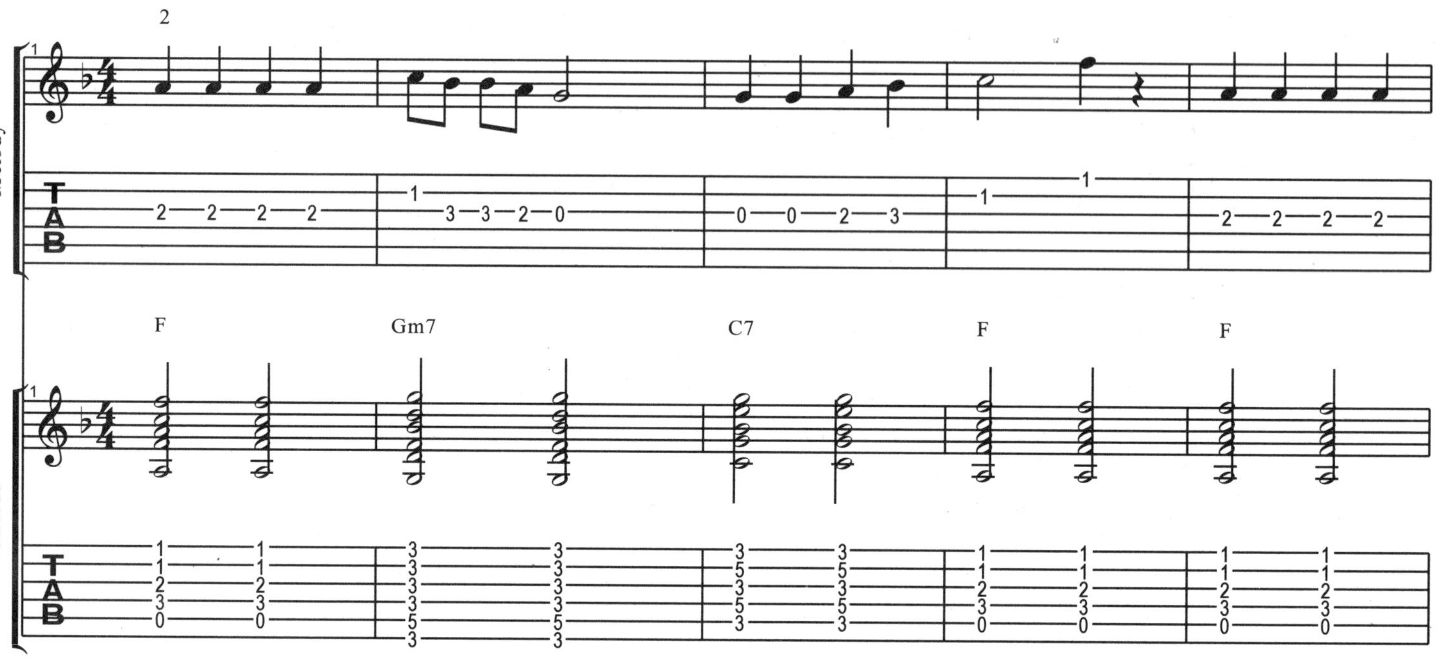

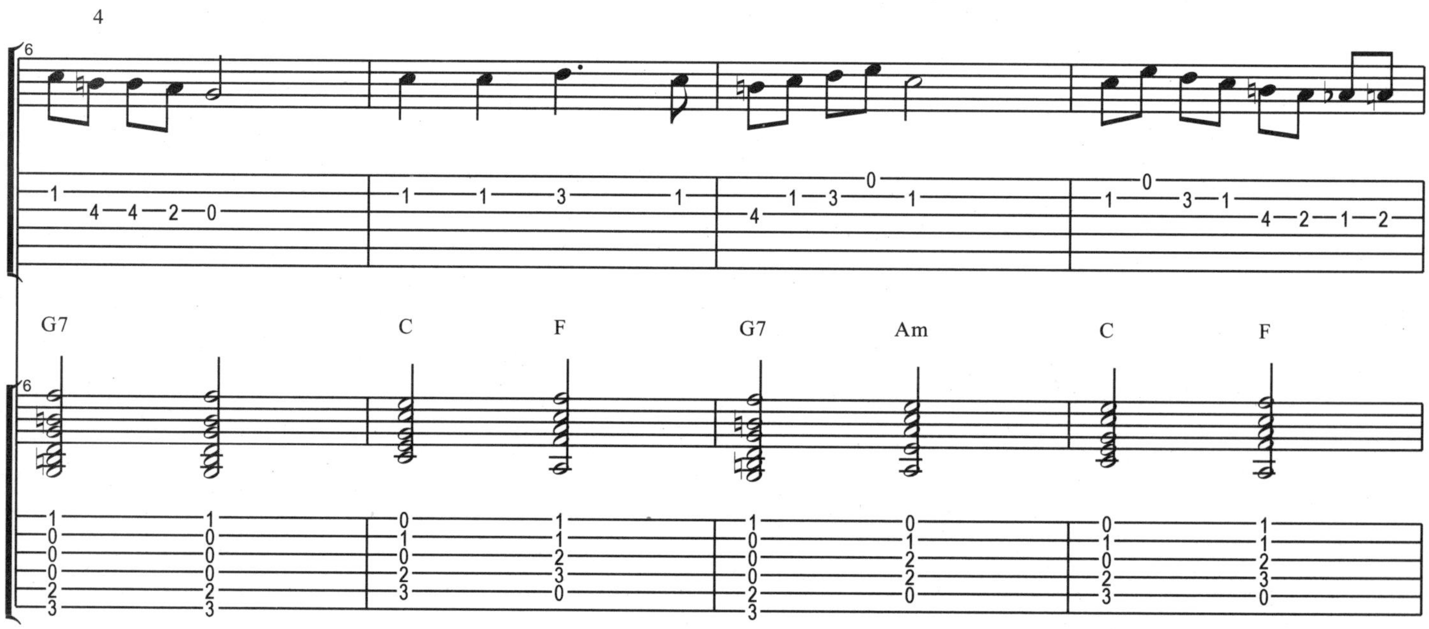

Melody
Chords
G7 C C C7 F Bb Gm7
Melody
Chords
F C7 F Bb Gm7 F C7 F

Rise To Death

Plectrum Guitar

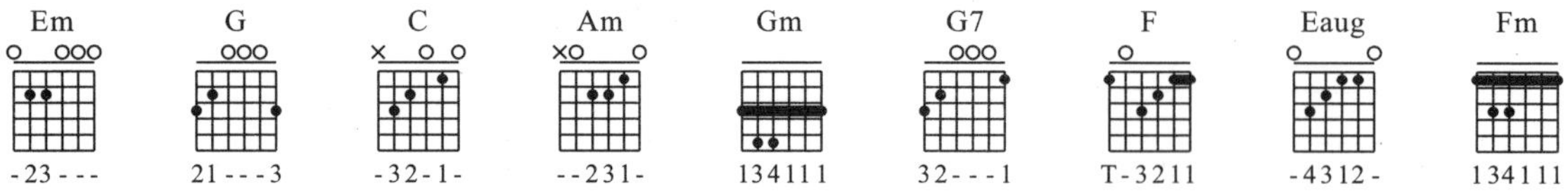

Melody
Chords
C C G7 G7 G7 G7 Em Em C C
Melody
Chords
C C Am Am F F Am Am Eaug Eaug Fm Fm

Melody
Chords
C C C C G7 G7 G7 G7 C

Yellow rose of Texas

Plectrum Guitar, Guitarmonk

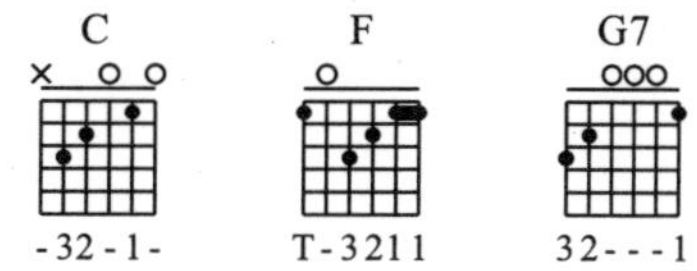

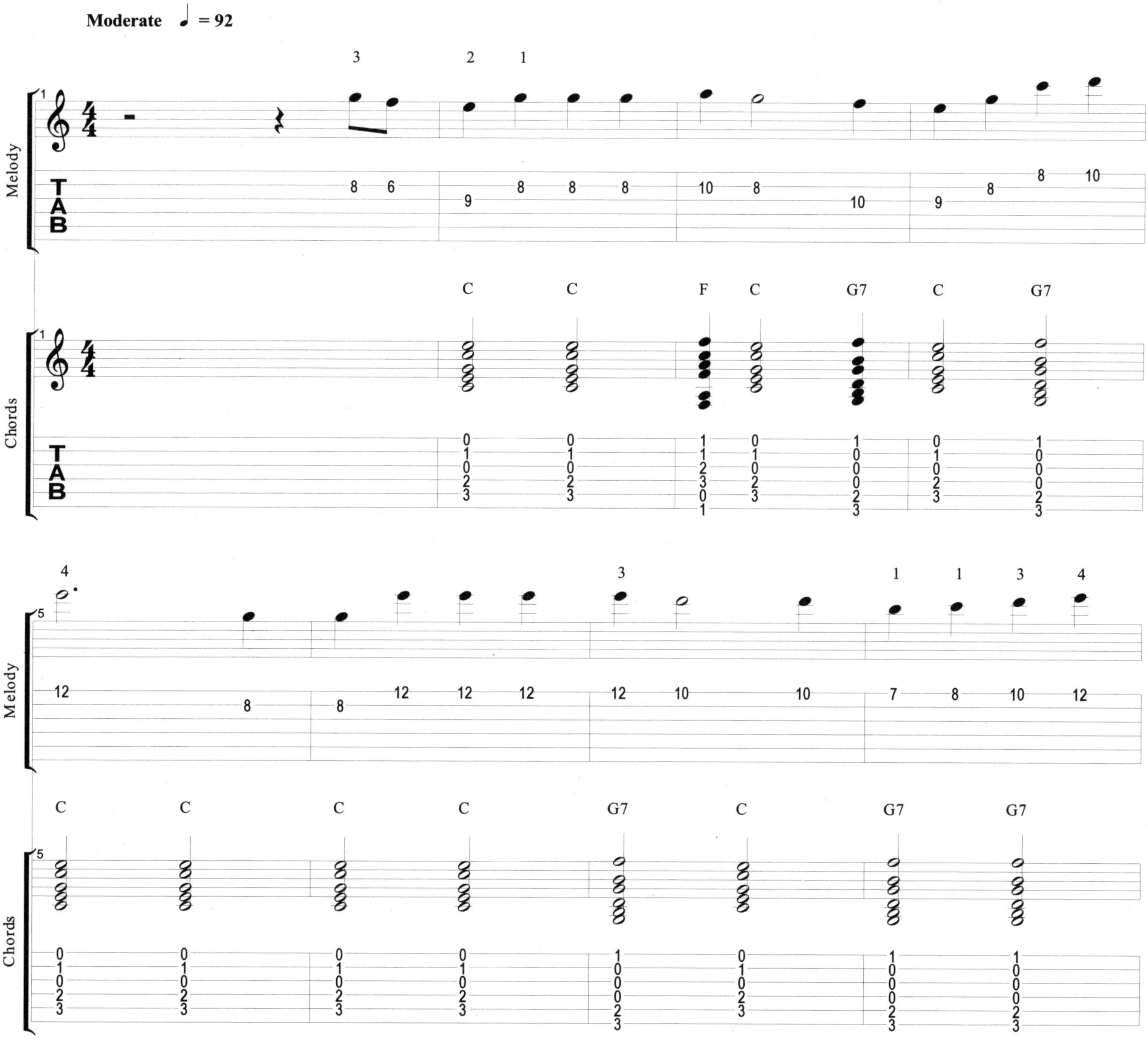

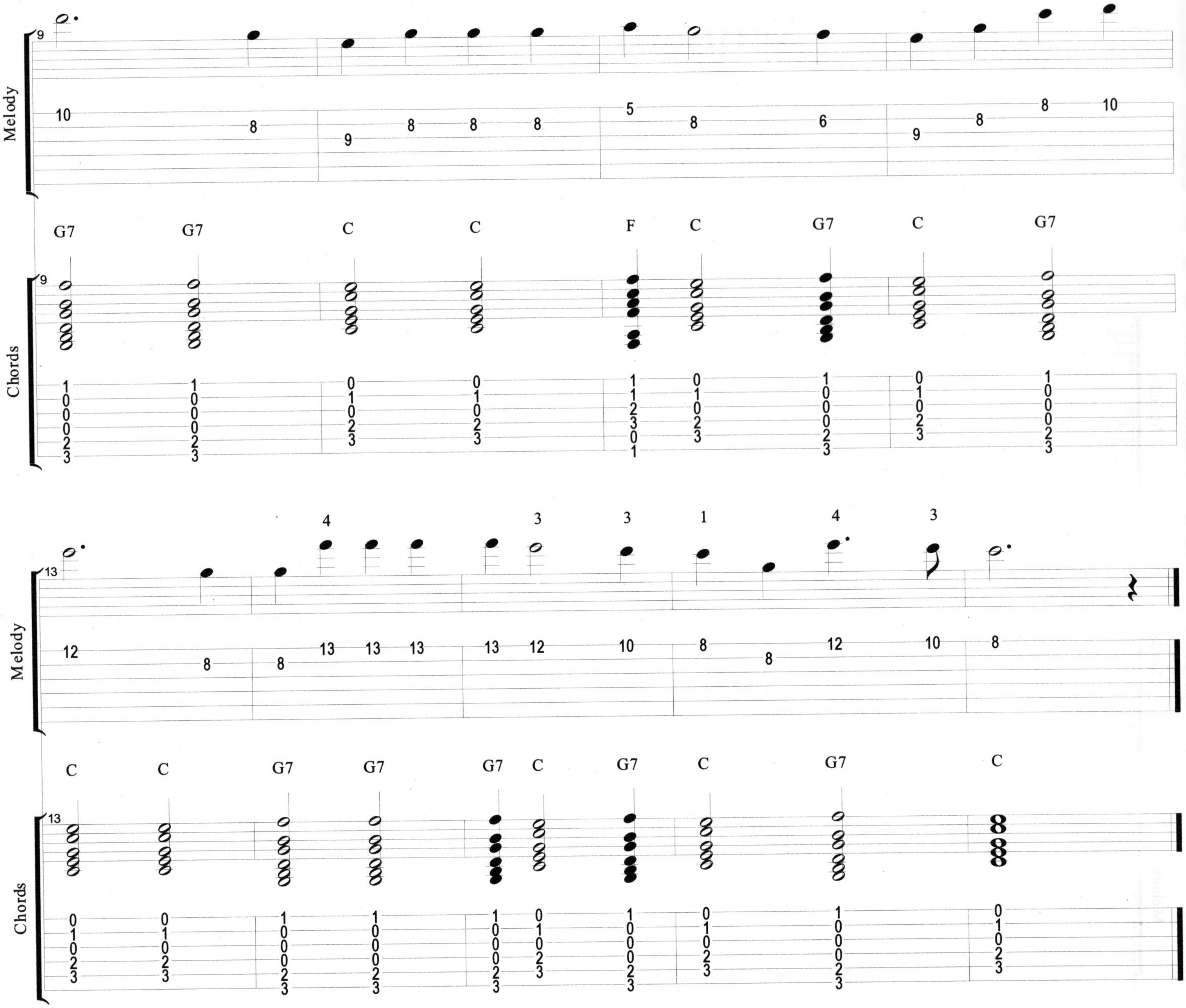
Melody
G7 G7 C C F C G7 C G7
Chords
Melody
C C G7 G7 G7 C G7 C G7 C
Chords

Worried Man Blues

Plectrum Guitar

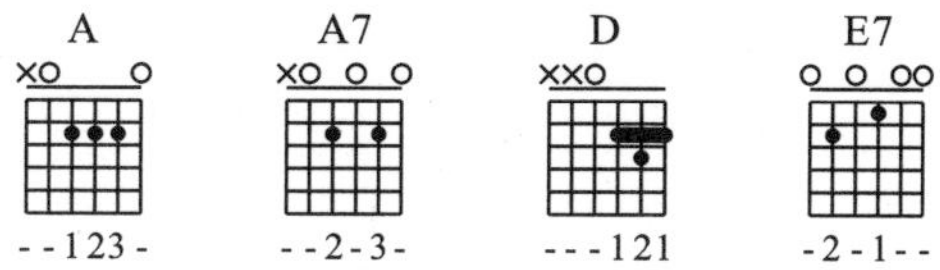

Melody
Chords
A A A A A A A A
E7 E7 E7 E7 A D D A

Do, Lord

Plectrum Guitar

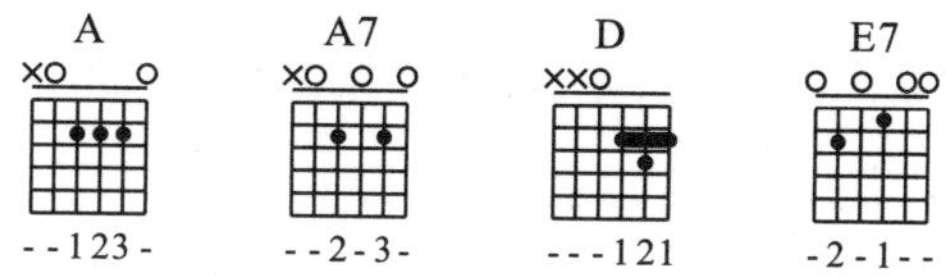

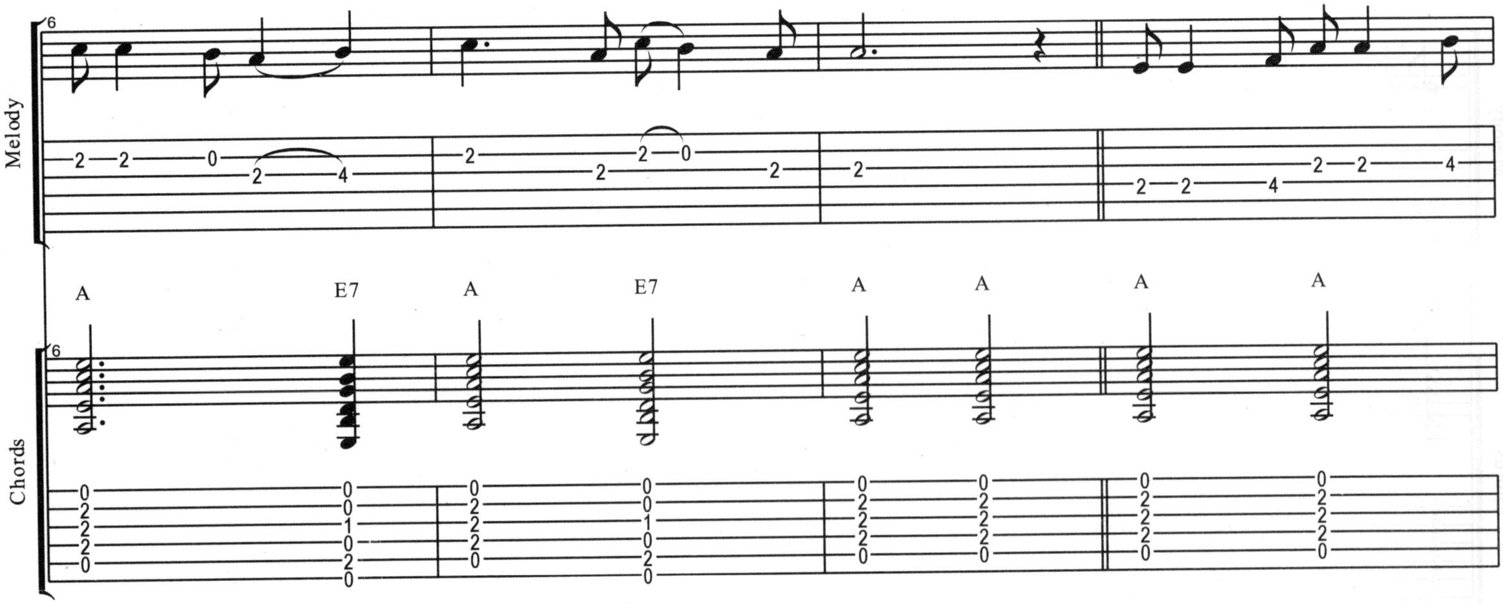
Melody
Chords
A E7 A E7 A A A A

Melody
Chords
A A7 D D D A

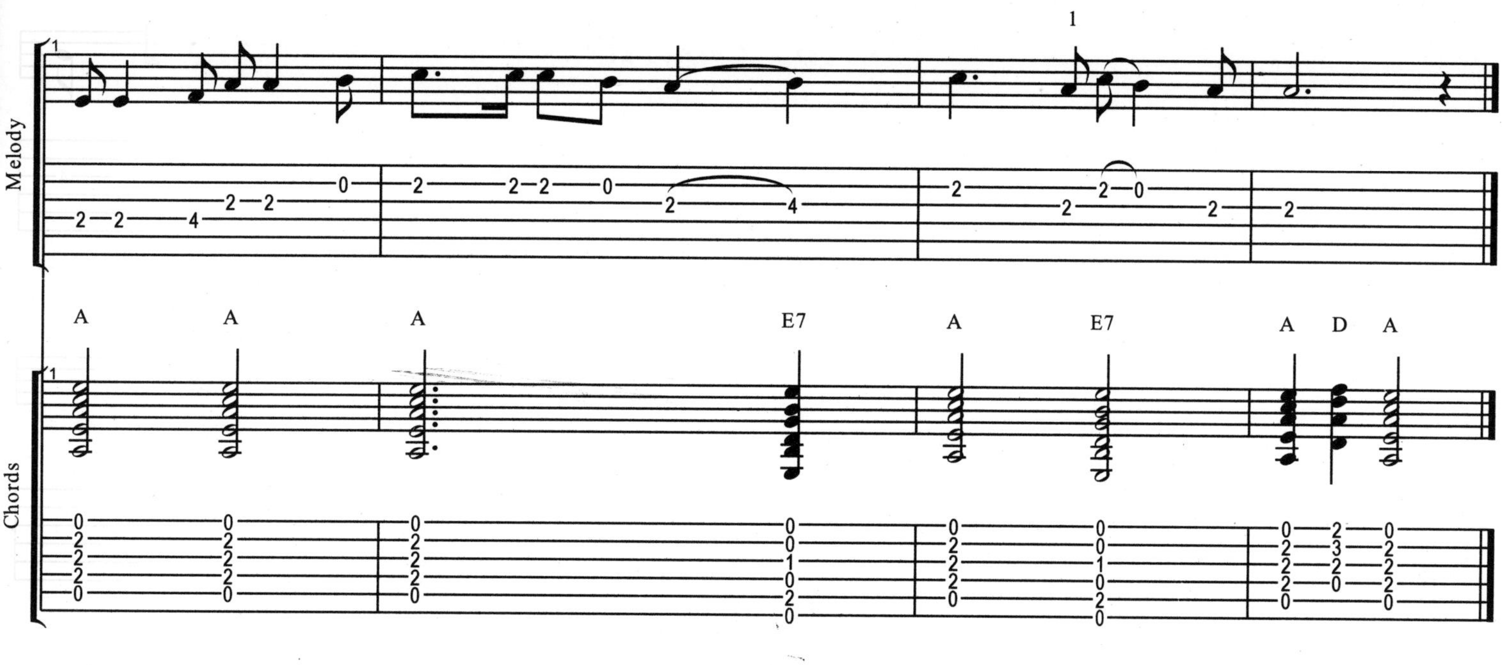
Melody
Chords
A A A E7 A E7 A D A

Little Lamb

Plectrum Guitar

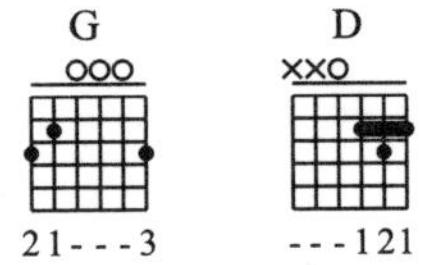

Moderate ♩ = 140

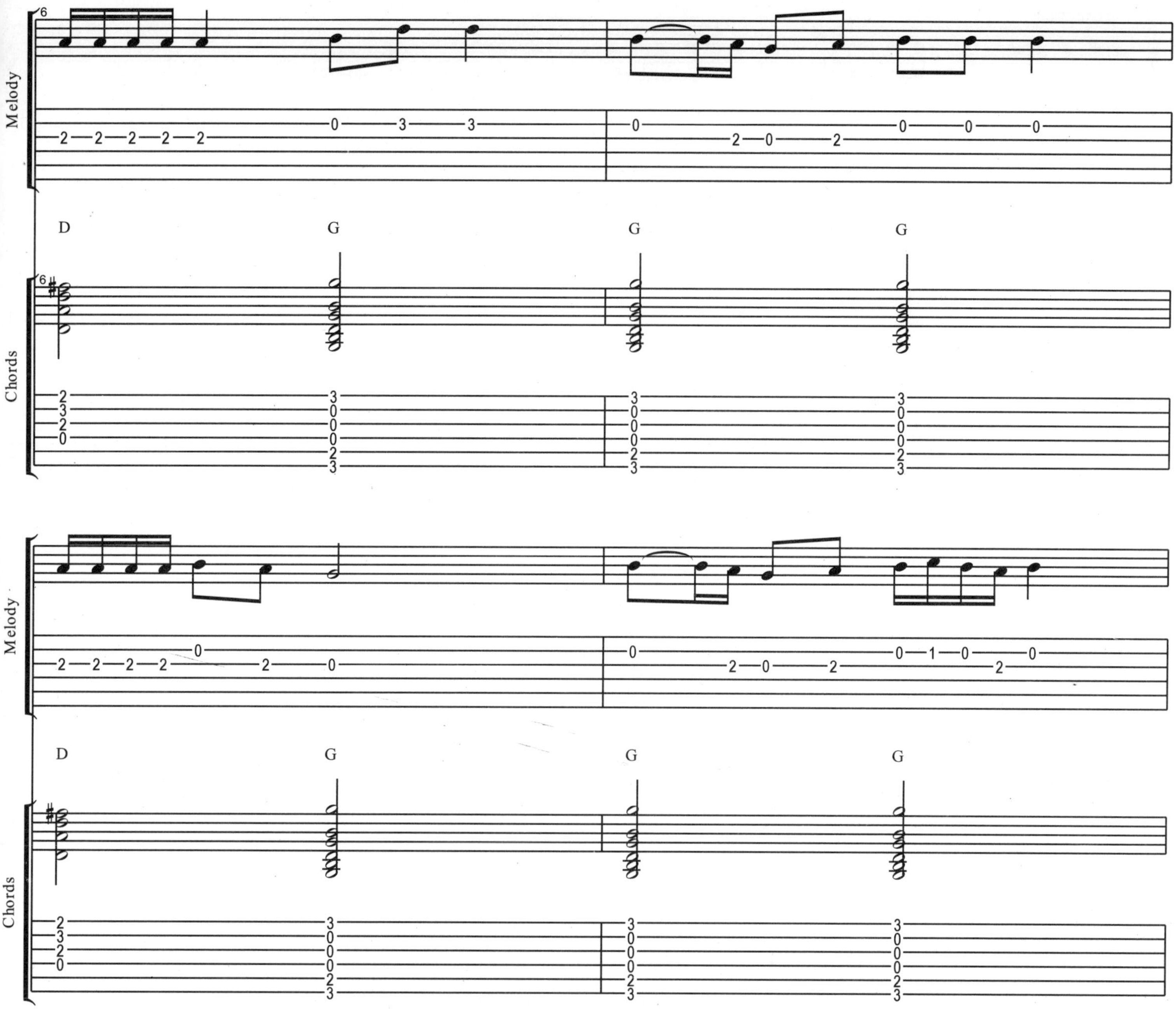
6
Melody
D
G
G
G
Chords
Melody
D
G
G
G
Chords

Melody
Chords
D
G
G
G
D
G

The Apple Blossom

Plectrum Guitar, Guitarmonk

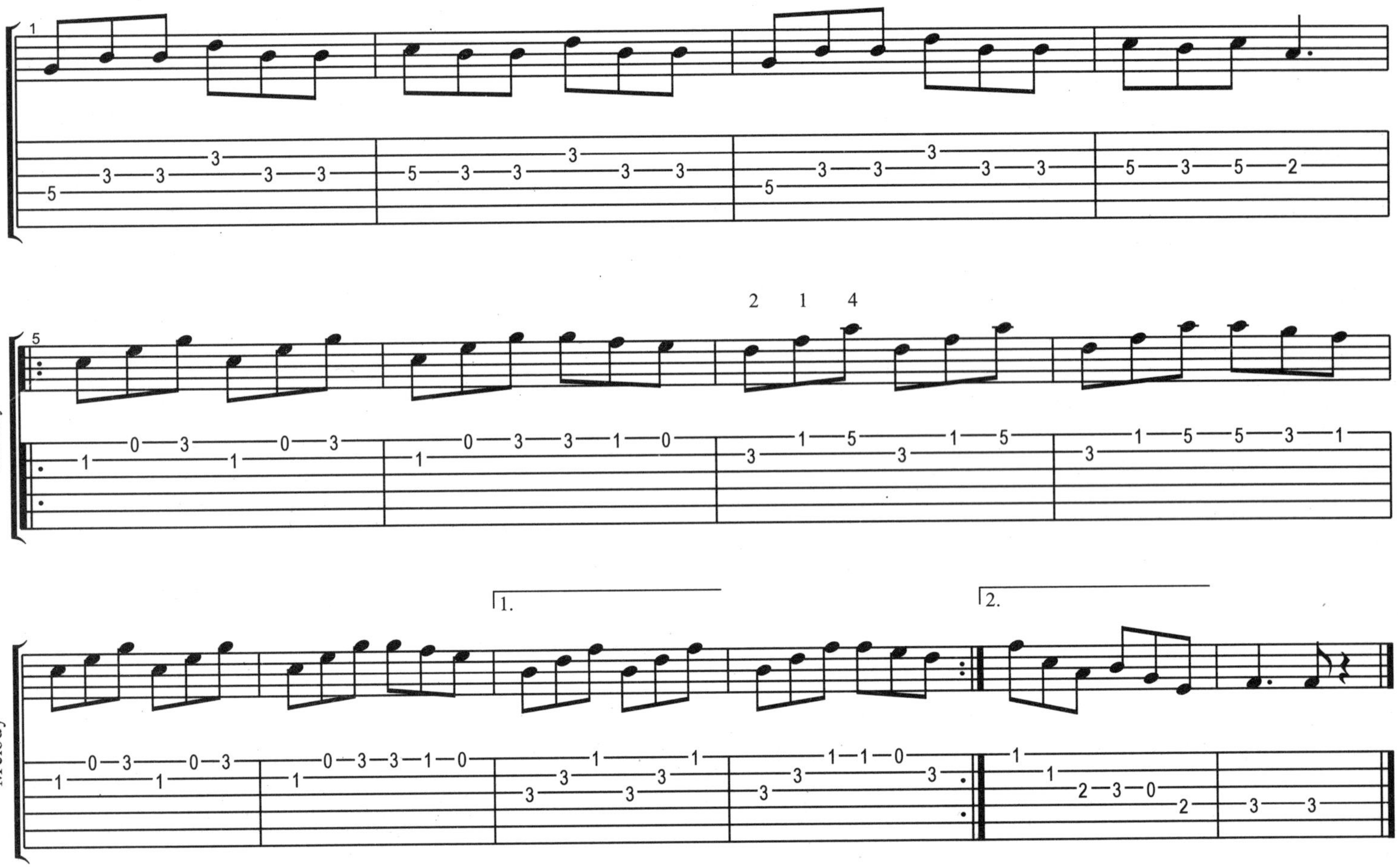
Melody
Melody
2 1 4
Melody
1.
2.

When Johnny Comes Marching Home

Plectrum Guitar

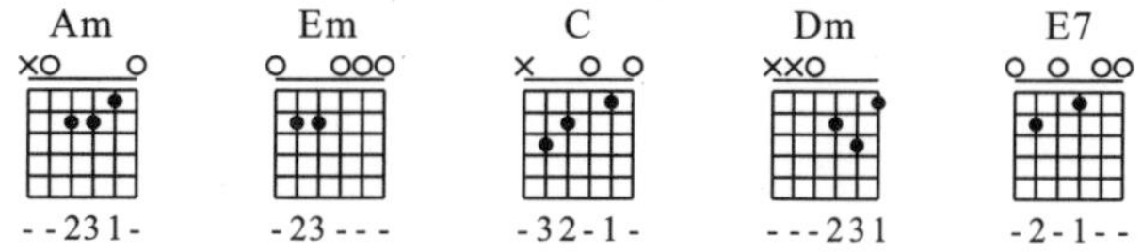

Melody
Chords
Dm
Am
E7
Am
E7
Melody
Chords
Am
E7
Am
Am

Western Pop Songs

MUSIC CHORDS AND LYRICS

(A beautiful repertoire for all music lovers and students...)

WESTERN SONGS

1. Love will Keep us alive
2. That's why you go away
3. Shape of my heart
4. Someday
5. She is always a woman to me
6. Can you feel the love tonight
7. Careless Whisper
8. Power of Love

LOVE WILL KEEP US ALIVE

1

Artist: Eagles
Album: Hell Freezes Over
Scale: A Major

A **F#m**
I was standin', all alone against the world outside
D **E**
You were searching for a place to hide
A **F#m**
Lost and lonely, now you've given me the will to survive
D **E** **A**
When we're hungry, love will keep us alive.

A **F#m**
Don't you worry; sometime you've gotta let it ride
D **E**
The world is changing, right before our eyes
A **F#m**
Girl I found you, there's no more emptiness inside
D **E** **A**
When we're hungry, love will keep us alive.

A **F#m**
Now I've found you there's no more emptiness inside
D **E** **A**
When we're hungry, love will keep us alive.

D
I would die for you,
F#m
Climb the highest mountain.
B **E**
Baby, there's nothin' I wouldn't do

I was standing,
All alone,
Against the world outside,
You were searching,
For a place to hide,
Lost and lonely,
Now you have given,
Me the will to survive,
When we're hungry,
Love will keep us alive...,

THAT'S WHY YOU GO AWAY

Artist: MLTR
Album: That's why you go away
Scale: A minor

```
Am                        D             G               G/B
Baby won't you tell me why; there is sadness in your eyes?
Am                       B        Em
I don't wanna say goodbye, to you
Am                D      D/F#            G
Love is one big illusion; I should try to forget
    A                      Dsus4    G
But there is something left in my head.

Am                          D          G                          G/B
You're the one who set it up, now you're the one to make it stop
Am                           B          Em
I'm the one who's feeling just right now
Am                           B  D/F#                  G
Now you want me to forget; every little thing you said
    A                      Dsus4    G
But there is something left in my head

Am                      D       G            G/B
You were never satisfy, no matter ho I tried
Am                       B       Em
Now you want to goodbye, to me
Am                D      D/F#            G
Love is one big illusion; I should try to forget
    A                      Dsus4    G
But there is something left in my head.

              C       D        G
I won't forget, the way your kisses
               Am           D           G
Feeling is strong, were lasting for so long.
                    C          D          Em
But I'm not the man; your heart is missing
                    Am D    G
That's why you go away I know
```

I won't forget,

The way your kisses,

Feeling is strong,

Were lasting for so long,

But I'm not the man,

Your heart is missing,

That's why you go,

Away I know,

SHAPE OF MY HEART

3

Artist: Backstreet Boys
Album: Black and Blue
Scale: D Major

```
D                           A        G
Baby, please try to forgive me
D                           A       G
Stay here, don't put out the glow
D
Hold me now, don't bother
           A                      G
If every minute makes me weaker
          Bm                              E
You can save me from the man that I become
G
Oh yeah

D
Sadness is beautiful
A               G
Loneliness is tragical
   D               A        G
So help me, I can't win this war, Oh no
D
Touch me now don't bother
           A                      G
If every second makes me weaker
          Bm                            E
You can save me from the man I've become

D                               G
Looking back on the things I've done
        A                 Fm
I was trying to be someone
              Bm
I played my part
                     E
And kept you in the dark
          G                        Fm      D
Now let me show you the shape of my heart
```

I'm looking back,

On things I've done,

I never wanna play,

The same old part,

And keep you in the dark,

Now let me show you,

The shape of my heart...,

SOMEDAY

Artist: MLTR
Album: Paint My Love
Scale: D Major

Bm G D A
In my search for freedom and peace of mind
Bm G D A Bm G
I've left the memories behind, wanna start a new life
D A E
But it seems to be rather absurd
G
When I know the truth
A
Is that I always think of you

Bm G D A
Try to throw the picture out of my mind
Bm G D A Bm G
Try to leave the memories behind, Here by the ocean
D A E
Wave's carry voice from you
G
Do you know the truth?
A
I am thinking of you too

When I know the truth,
Is that I always think of you,
Someday someway
Together we will be baby,
I will take and,
You will take your time,
We'll wait for our fate,
'Cause nobody owns us baby,

C
The love we had together
G/B
Just fade away in time
Gm/Bb
And now you've got your own world
C D
And I guess I've got mine
C
But the passion that you planted
G/B
In the middle of my heart
Gm/Bb A
Is a passion that will never stop

D A
Someday someway
Bm G
Together we will be baby
D Bm A
I will take and you will take your time
D A
We'll wait for our fate
Bm G
'Cause nobody owns us baby
D A D
We can shake we can shake the rock

SHE ALWAYS A WOMAN TO ME

5

Artist: Billy Joel
Album: The Stranger
Scale: D Major

```
        A7         D                 A7                 D
She can kill with a smile; She can wound with her eyes,
                    G                Bm     G
She can ruin your faith with her casual lies,
        A7    D                  A7               F#
And she only reveals what she wants you to see,
   Bm                             G          A7         D
She hides like a child but she's always a woman to me
```

She can lead you to love; She can take you on leaving,
She can ask for the truth, but you'll never believe,
She takes what you'll give her as long as it's free,
Yes, she steals like a thief but she's always a woman to me.

She promises you more than Garden of Eden,
And, then she'll carelessly cut you, and laugh while you're bleeding,
But you bring out the best, then the worst you can be,
Blame it all on your self, but she's always a woman to me.

Hmm ... Hmm ... Hmm...

She frequently kind,

She's suddenly cool,

She can do as she pleases,

She's nobody's fool,

And she can't be conducted,

She's earned her degree,

And the most she will do,

Is throw shadows to you,

```
Bm   E7                   A     F#m          D          Gs
  Oh! She takes care of herself;    she can wait if she wants,
Em       A7
  She's ahead of her time.
Dm        G7                C    Am                  Bm
  Oh! And she never gives out and she never gives in,
E7                       A7
 She just changes her mind.
```

CAN YOU FEEL THE LOVE TONIGHT

Eb Bb Eb Bb
There's a calm surrender, To the rush of day.
Eb Dm
When the heat of a rolling world
Cm F7
Can be turned away,
Eb Bb Eb Bb
An enchanted moment, and it seems me through
Eb Gm
It's enough for this restless warrior
Ab F7
Just to be with you.

Eb Bb Eb Bb
There's a time for everyone, If they only learn
Eb Dm
That the twisting kaleidoscope,
Cm F7
Move us all in turn,
Eb Bb Eb Bb
There's a rhyme and reason, to the world outdoors
Eb Gm
When the heart of this star-crossed voyager
Ab F7
Beats in time with yours

Bb Gm Eb
And can you feel the love tonight?
Bb Eb E F7
It is where we are
Eb Gm F7 Eb
It's enough for this wide-eyed wonderer
Cm Dm Eb F7
That we got this far
Bb Gm Eb
And can you feel the love tonight?
Bb Eb E F7
How it's laid to rest?
Eb Gm F7 Eb
It's enough to make kings and vagabonds
Cm Dm Eb Bb
Believe the very best.

Artist: Elton John
Album: The Lion King
Scale: Eb Major

And can you feel,

The love tonight?

It is where we are,

It's enough,

For this wide-eyed wonderer,

That we got this far.,

CARELESS WHISPER

Artist: George Michael
Album: Ladies & Gentleman
Scale: D minor

Dm Gm
I feel so unsure.
Bb Am
As I take your hand and lead you to the dance floor.
Dm
As the music dies,
Gm
Something in your eyes,
Bb
Calls to mind a silver screen,
Am
And you're its sad goodbye.

Dm
Tonight the music seems so loud
Gm
I wish that we could loose this crowd,
Bb
Maybe, it's better this way
Am
We'd hurt each other with the thing we want to say
Dm
It could have been so good together,
Gm
We could have lived this dance forever
Bb Am...
Now who's gonna dance with me

Time can never mend,

The careless whisper,

Of a good friend.

To the heart and mind,

Ignorance is kind.

There's no comfort,

In the truth,

Pain is all you'll find,

Dm
I'm never gonna dance again,
Gm
Guilty feet have got no rhythm,
Bb
Though it's easy to pretend,
Am
I know you're not a fool.
Dm
I should have known better than to cheat a friend,
Gm
And waste a chance that I've been given,
Bb Am
So I'm never gonna dance again, the way I dance with you.

POWER OF LOVE

Artist: Celine Dion
Album: The color of my life
Scale: A Major

```
       A                               F#m
The whispers in the morning, of lovers sleeping fight
                     A                         E
Are rolling like thunder now, as I look in your eyes
               A                         F#m
I hold on to your body, and fell each move you make
                    D                        A          E
Your voices is warm and tender, a love that I could not forsake

              A
Cause I'm your lady
               D
And you are my man
               Bm
Whenever you reach for me
         E
I'll do all that I can.

                A
We're heading for something
               D
Somewhere I've never been
               Bm
Sometimes I am frightened
               E
But I'm ready to learn
          A
Of power of love

              D                            Bm
Sometimes the power of love, sometimes I am frightened
               E           A
But I'm ready to learn, of the power of love

Power of love...
```

Cause I'm your lady,

And you are my man,

Whenever you reach for me,

I'll do all that I can,

Sometimes I am frightened,

But I'm ready to learn,

Of power of love,